JESUS

Is Most

SPECIAL

JESUS
Is Most
SPECIAL

by Sally Michael

Illustrations by Fred Apps

P&R
PUBLISHING
P.O. BOX 817 • PHILLIPSBURG • NEW JERSEY 08865-0817

Scripture quotations are from *ESV Bible* ® (*The Holy Bible, English Standard Version* ®). Copyright © 2001 by Crossway Bibles, a publishing ministry of Good News Publishers. Used by permission. All rights reserved.

ISBN: 978-1-62995-029-7 (hc)
ISBN: 978-1-62995-030-3 (ePub)
ISBN: 978-1-62995-031-0 (Mobi)

Textured background © istockphoto.com / flas100

Cover, page design, and typesetting by Dawn Premako

Printed in the United States of America

Library of Congress Control Number: 2014937824

You shall call his name Jesus, for he
will save his people from their sins.
—*Matthew 1:21*

A WORD TO PARENTS

This book was written to help parents share the wonderful story of the birth of the Savior with their children so that they, in turn, will be able to retell it to others. Though the facts are important for children to remember, it is even more important for them to understand the message of the birth of Christ, God's Son, the Savior of the world, the King of all Kings, who is most special of all.

How to Use This Book

- Read the story several times to your child.
- Start with the title and main story text on each right-hand page. After you have read this section of the story with your child, use the Scripture or song quotation on the opposite page to further reinforce what you have learned, to reflect on its meaning, and to stir your heart to worship.
- Practice the story over a period of days. Read the title of each section and encourage your child to tell you the text of that section, at first with your help.
- Practice the story until your child is able to tell the story without help, or with minimal help. The story may be told using the book or using a nativity set. Each figure, in turn, can be added to the nativity set at the point in the story indicated by this symbol: ✳. A note at the bottom of each

story will indicate which figure or figures correspond with the symbol.

- Encourage your child to tell the Christmas story to the family on Christmas Eve or Christmas Day as you celebrate the birth of the Savior and the true meaning of Christmas.

This Christmas, may you and your children worship Jesus, the Savior of the world, the King of Kings, who is most special of all.

For to us a child is born,
to us a son is given;
and the government shall be
  upon his shoulder,
and his name shall be called
Wonderful Counselor, Mighty God,
Everlasting Father, Prince of Peace.
—Isaiah 9:6

❧ PROMISE ❧

God made a promise to His people. He would send a Savior to take the punishment for their sin.

O come, O come, Emmanuel,
And ransom captive Israel,
That mourns in lonely exile here
Until the Son of God appear.
Rejoice! Rejoice! Emmanuel
shall come to thee, O Israel.

❧ WAITING ❧

So the Jews were waiting and waiting and waiting . . . for a long, long time. Waiting for a Savior. Waiting for a King. Waiting for the "Lamb of God" to take away their sins. Waiting for . . . Jesus.

And behold, you will conceive in your womb and bear a son, and you shall call his name Jesus. He will be great and will be called the Son of the Most High. And the Lord God will give to him the throne of his father David, and he will reign over the house of Jacob forever, and of his kingdom there will be no end.

—Luke 1:31–33

❧ MARY ❧

Mary was waiting, too. ✳ But then an angel came and said that the time had come—Jesus would be born! Mary would have a baby—a special baby, God's Son.

✳ *Mary* (Note: see "A Word to Parents" for the best approach to reading each story.)

And Joseph also went up . . . to the city of David, which is called Bethlehem . . . with Mary, his betrothed, who was with child. And while they were there, the time came for her to give birth. And she gave birth to her firstborn son and wrapped him in swaddling cloths and laid him in a manger, because there was no place for them in the inn.
—Luke 2:4–7

❧ BETHLEHEM ❧

Mary and Joseph went to Bethlehem, where God said Jesus would be born. ✳ There was no room for Jesus in the inn house with the other people—no room except in the place with the animals. ✳✳

✳ *Joseph/donkey*
✳✳ *Stable*

Away in a manger, no crib for a bed,
The little Lord Jesus laid down his sweet head.
The stars in the sky looked down where he lay,
The little Lord Jesus asleep in the hay.

✤ *JESUS* ✤

And right there with the animals, baby Jesus, God's Son, the King
of the World, was born! ✳

✳ *Jesus*

Joy to the world! the Lord is come;
Let earth receive her King;
Let every heart prepare him room,
And heaven and nature sing,
And heaven and nature sing,
And heaven, and heaven, and nature sing.

❧ SHEPHERDS ❧

Shepherds were watching their sheep near Bethlehem. ✳

They were waiting for Jesus, too. All of a sudden, there was an angel in the sky. ✳✳ And the shepherds were afraid!

But the angel said, "Don't be afraid! I have really good news! A Savior has been born! God's Son, the one who came to take away the sin of the world. You will find baby Jesus in a manger."

Suddenly the sky was filled with angels saying, "Glory to God in the highest!"

The shepherds went to find baby Jesus. They wanted to see the Savior, the baby who was the King of All . . . and they left worshiping God.

✳ *Shepherds/sheep*
✳✳ *Angel*

Now after Jesus was born in Bethlehem of Judea in the days of Herod the king, behold, wise men from the east came to Jerusalem, saying, "Where is he who has been born king of the Jews? For we saw his star when it rose and have come to worship him."
—Matthew 2:1–2

❧ WISE MEN ❧

Later, wise men from far away saw a special light in the sky. ✳
"The King of the Jews has been born," they said. They followed
the light, looking for King Jesus, born as a little baby. The light led
them right to Jesus.

   The wise men brought gifts for Jesus. They bowed down and
worshiped King Jesus. Jesus is the most special of all. Jesus is the
Son of God. Jesus is the Savior who came to take away our sin.
Jesus is the King of all Kings!

✳ Kings/star/camel

Go, tell it on the mountain,
Over the hills and everywhere.
Go, tell it on the mountain
That Jesus Christ is born.

❧ *TELL* ❧

Some people still don't know about Jesus, God's Son, the Savior of the World. Some people don't worship Him—they don't love Him and bow down to Him as King Jesus. They don't know that Jesus is most special of all.

We must tell them about Jesus, the Savior for all kinds of people, who is the most special of all.

The true light, which enlightens everyone, was coming into the world. He was in the world, and the world was made through him, yet the world did not know him. He came to his own, and his own people did not receive him. But to all who did receive him, who believed in his name, he gave the right to become children of God, who were born, not of blood nor of the will of the flesh nor of the will of man, but of God.

—*John 1:9–13*